# Adding with Sebastian Pig and Friends
## At the Circus

By Jill Anderson

Illustrated by Amy Huntington

Series Math Consultant:
Cassi Heppelmann
Elementary School Teacher
Farmington School District
Minnesota

Series Literacy Consultant:
Allan A. De Fina, Ph.D.
Dean, College of Education / Professor of Literacy Education
New Jersey City University
Past President of the New Jersey Reading Association

**Enslow Elementary**
an imprint of
**Enslow Publishers, Inc.**
40 Industrial Road
Box 398
Berkeley Heights, NJ 07922
USA

http://www.enslow.com

**To Parents and Teachers:**

As you read Sebastian's story with a child,

   *Rely on the pictures to see the math visually represented.

   *Use Sebastian's notebook, which summarizes the math at hand.

   *Practice math facts with your child using the charts at the end of this book.

Enslow Elementary, an imprint of Enslow Publishers, Inc.

Enslow Elementary® is a registered trademark of Enslow Publishers, Inc.

Copyright © 2009 by Enslow Publishers, Inc.

**Library of Congress Cataloging-in-Publication Data**
Anderson, Jill, 1968-
  Adding with Sebastian pig and friends : at the circus / written by Jill Anderson ; illustrated by Amy Huntington.
    p. cm. — (Math fun with Sebastian pig and friends!)
  Includes index.
  Summary: "A fun review of addition for beginning readers"—Provided by publisher.
  ISBN-13: 978-0-7660-3360-3
  ISBN-10: 0-7660-3360-0
  1. Addition—Juvenile literature. I. Title.
QA115.A53 2009
513.2'11—dc22
                    2008028470

Editorial Direction: Red Line Editorial, Inc.

Printed in the United States of America

10 9 8 7 6 5 4 3 2 1

To Our Readers: We have done our best to make sure all Internet Addresses in this book were active and appropriate when we went to press. However, the author and the publisher have no control and assume no liability for the material available on those Internet sites or on other Web sites they may link to. Any comments or suggestions can be sent by e-mail to comments@enslow.com or to the address on the back cover.

Enslow Publishers, Inc. is committed to printing our books on recycled paper. The paper in every book contains 10% to 30% post-consumer waste (PCW). The cover board on the outside of every book contains 100% PCW. Our goal is to do our part to help young people and the environment too!

# Table of Contents

# Sebastian at the Circus

Lucky Sebastian Pig! Today he is going to the circus. He has a big job to do. Help Sebastian add. Need help? Look for the answers in Sebastian's notebook.

6

Ladies and animals!

Let the circus begin!

Everyone is ready!

### Zip, Zoom . . . Clowns!

Honk, honk! A clown zooms into the ring. He goes around and around.

Three more clowns drive in.

Sebastian writes it all down. First there is one clown, then three more. Wow! That's adding. Sebastian writes **1 + 3 = □**

How many are there?

Look! Two elephants skate into the ring.
Add elephants to clowns. What you get is . . . CRASH!

How many are there?

11

You can add
by counting on!

4 + 2 = 6

# Monkeys Show Off

Look up! Three monkeys show off. Four more monkeys come in. They flip and fly.

How many monkeys are there?

Add the monkeys!

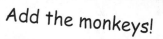

$3 + 4 = 7$

The answer is called the sum.

Now two hippos come in. Sebastian adds monkeys
plus hippos. Or should it be hippos plus monkeys?
He writes the problem both ways. How many are there?

Monkeys + Hippos

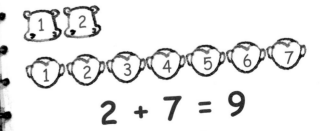

$$7 + 2 = 9$$

Hippos + Monkeys

$$2 + 7 = 9$$

The sums are the same.

# Fancy Horses and Riders

Five fancy horses with five riders enter the ring. The number of horses and riders is the same. How many are there?

18

What is that bear doing? High above the ground, she turns on her toes.

Uh-oh! The bear is falling. Sebastian adds the bear to the 10 horses and riders. How many are there now?

Plus one bear. . .

1 2 3 4 5 6 7 8 9 10

1

**10 + 1 = 11**

You can add more than 10!

# Lots of Big Cats

Four tigers toss balls and bowling pins. Then eight lions come in. Sebastian adds up all the big cats. How many are there?

Tigers + Lions

4 + 8 = 12

A group of twelve is a dozen.

Fire! Fire! Four hedgehogs run in with hoses. They put out the fire. But the dozen big cats do not stop. Sebastian adds the hedgehogs to the big cats. How many are there?

Add even more by counting on!

1 2 3 4 5 6 7 8 9 10 11 12
13 14 15 16

# 12 + 4 = 16

The numbers you add
together are called addends.

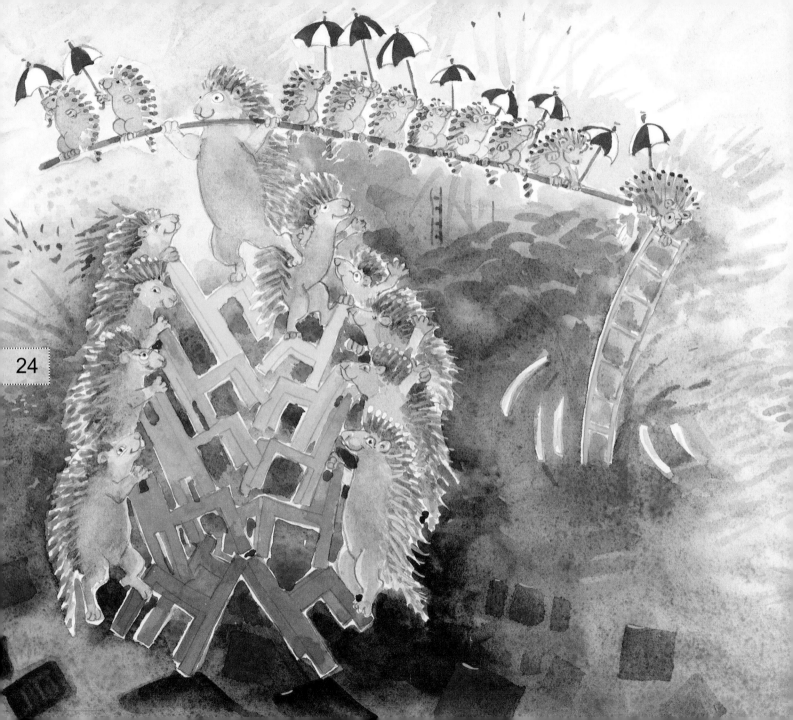

24

# Porcupines Everywhere!

It is the end of the show. It is time for the porcupines. Ten porcupines are everywhere. Then their ten children come in. How many porcupines are there?

Add doubles!

1 2 3 4 5 6 7 8 9 10
1 2 3 4 5 6 7 8 9 10

## 10 + 10 = 20
Do you remember which number doubles to make 10?

The gorilla comes in. He wants to be part of the act.
The 20 porcupines will jump off his belly.
How many animals are there?

26

There are 21 animals!

| 1 | 2 | 3 | 4 | 5 | 6 | 7 | 8 | 9 | 10 |

| 11 | 12 | 13 | 14 | 15 | 16 | 17 | 18 | 19 | 20 |

1

20 + 1 = 21

**Boom!**

One by one, the porcupines fall. Everyone runs to help.

Even Sebastian gets into the act. But he falls into the cannon. Boom! He is part of the show. Sebastian has a great story to tell. His story will be the best one.

# Now You Know

Good work! You helped Sebastian add all of the animals.
Use this chart to practice more addition facts!

## + 0

0 + 0 = 0
1 + 0 = 1
2 + 0 = 2
3 + 0 = 3
4 + 0 = 4
5 + 0 = 5
6 + 0 = 6
7 + 0 = 7
8 + 0 = 8
9 + 0 = 9
10 + 0 = 10

## + 1

0 + 1 = 1
1 + 1 = 2
2 + 1 = 3
3 + 1 = 4
4 + 1 = 5
5 + 1 = 6
6 + 1 = 7
7 + 1 = 8
8 + 1 = 9
9 + 1 = 10
10 + 1 = 11

## + 2

0 + 2 = 2
1 + 2 = 3
2 + 2 = 4
3 + 2 = 5
4 + 2 = 6
5 + 2 = 7
6 + 2 = 8
7 + 2 = 9
8 + 2 = 10
9 + 2 = 11
10 + 2 = 12

## + 3

0 + 3 = 3
1 + 3 = 4
2 + 3 = 5
3 + 3 = 6
4 + 3 = 7
5 + 3 = 8
6 + 3 = 9
7 + 3 = 10
8 + 3 = 11
9 + 3 = 12
10 + 3 = 13

## + 4

0 + 4 = 4
1 + 4 = 5
2 + 4 = 6
3 + 4 = 7
4 + 4 = 8
5 + 4 = 9
6 + 4 = 10
7 + 4 = 11
8 + 4 = 12
9 + 4 = 13
10 + 4 = 14

## + 5

0 + 5 = 5
1 + 5 = 6
2 + 5 = 7
3 + 5 = 8
4 + 5 = 9
5 + 5 = 10
6 + 5 = 11
7 + 5 = 12
8 + 5 = 13
9 + 5 = 14
10 + 5 = 15

## + 6

0 + 6 = 6
1 + 6 = 7
2 + 6 = 8
3 + 6 = 9
4 + 6 = 10
5 + 6 = 11
6 + 6 = 12
7 + 6 = 13
8 + 6 = 14
9 + 6 = 15
10 + 6 = 16

## + 7

0 + 7 = 7
1 + 7 = 8
2 + 7 = 9
3 + 7 = 10
4 + 7 = 11
5 + 7 = 12
6 + 7 = 13
7 + 7 = 14
8 + 7 = 15
9 + 7 = 16
10 + 7 = 17

## + 8

0 + 8 = 8
1 + 8 = 9
2 + 8 = 10
3 + 8 = 11
4 + 8 = 12
5 + 8 = 13
6 + 8 = 14
7 + 8 = 15
8 + 8 = 16
9 + 8 = 17
10 + 8 = 18

## + 9

0 + 9 = 9
1 + 9 = 10
2 + 9 = 11
3 + 9 = 12
4 + 9 = 13
5 + 9 = 14
6 + 9 = 15
7 + 9 = 16
8 + 9 = 17
9 + 9 = 18
10 + 9 = 19

## + 10

0 + 10 = 10
1 + 10 = 11
2 + 10 = 12
3 + 10 = 13
4 + 10 = 14
5 + 10 = 15
6 + 10 = 16
7 + 10 = 17
8 + 10 = 18
9 + 10 = 19
10 + 10 = 20

## Doubles

0 + 0 = 0
1 + 1 = 2
2 + 2 = 4
3 + 3 = 6
4 + 4 = 8
5 + 5 = 10
6 + 6 = 12
7 + 7 = 14
8 + 8 = 16
9 + 9 = 18
10 + 10 = 20

## Words to Know

**addend**—A number that is added to another number.
**doubles**—Two of the same number.
**dozen**—A group of twelve.
**sum**—The answer to an addition problem.

## Learn More

### Books

Cleary, Brian P. *The Mission of Addition*. Minneapolis, MN: Millbrook, 2005.

Murphy, Patricia J. *Adding Puppies and Kittens*. Berkeley Heights, NJ: Enslow Elementary, 2008.

Murphy, Stuart J. *Jack the Builder*. New York: HarperCollins, 2006.

### Web Sites

A Plus Math
www.aplusmath.com

Kids Numbers
http://www.kidsnumbers.com

## Index